GOD DOES MIRACLES

Four great stories from the Old Testament

CONTENTS

The Miracle of the Parting Waves	2
The Miracle of the Crumbling City	8
The Miracle of Naaman's Cure	14
The Miracle of the Fiery Furnace	22
The Miracle of God Today	30

Retold from Scripture by Claire Freedman
Illustrated by Arthur Baker

Kevin Mayhew

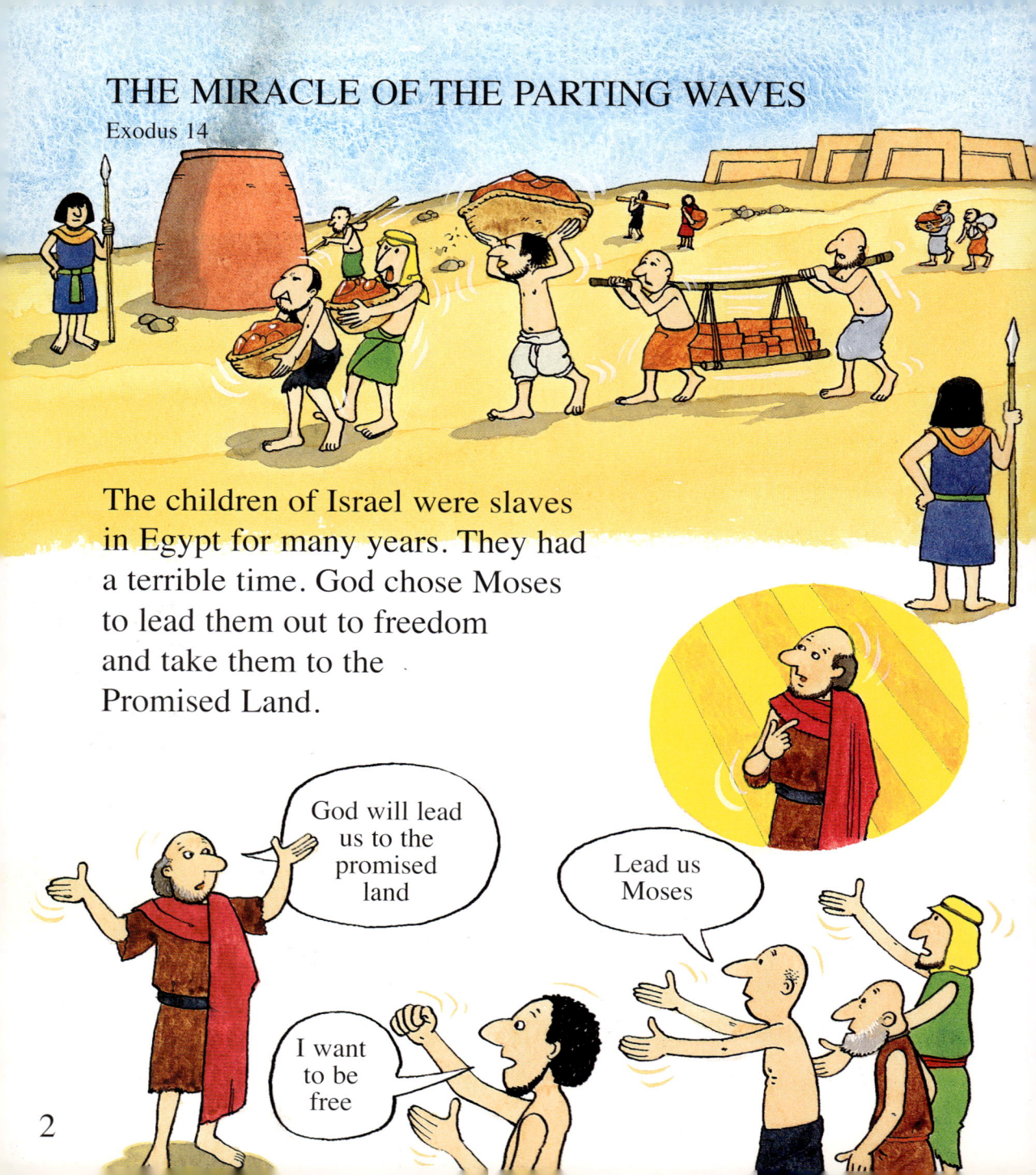

THE MIRACLE OF THE PARTING WAVES
Exodus 14

The children of Israel were slaves in Egypt for many years. They had a terrible time. God chose Moses to lead them out to freedom and take them to the Promised Land.

"God will lead us to the promised land"

"Lead us Moses"

"I want to be free"

At long last, after God had sent the Egyptians many plagues and disasters, the children of Israel were on their way, but suddenly, Pharaoh, the king of Egypt, changed his mind.

3

'I'm not letting the children of Israel go free after all,' he cried to his servants. 'Prepare my fastest chariots and best horsemen. Go and bring them back!'

When the children of Israel saw the Egyptian soldiers in their chariots catching them up, they were terrified. 'We're trapped,' they shouted. 'There's no way forward but the Red Sea.'

But Moses trusted God. 'God has promised to save us, and he will,' he told the people. God instructed Moses to stretch his hands out over the sea.
As Moses did so, the sea parted!
It made a dry path for the people to walk through.

'Now we can cross the sea safely!' the Israelites cheered.
But soon, the Egyptians followed! 'Stretch out your hands over the sea again,' God told Moses. This time the waters returned and the Egyptians were all drowned.
God had rescued his people.
What a miracle!

THE MIRACLE OF THE CRUMBLING CITY
Joshua 6:1-20

The children of Israel had been on a long journey to Canaan, the Promised Land.
Finally, they had arrived – and the first big city they came to was called Jericho.

"You can't get us!"

'God has promised to capture Jericho for us,'
Joshua, the leader, told the people.
However, there was a big problem.
No one could get inside Jericho.
The city walls were too high and thick
and its doors were tightly shut!

"Trust God – he will do it"

"It's too hard for us"

"It's hopeless"

"What shall we do?"

"We'll never get in"

'It's impossible to get in,' sighed the people. But God told Joshua, 'Nothing is impossible for me. Just follow my instructions. Let seven priests march once around the city each day, blowing trumpets, and tell your soldiers to march with them in silence. Do this for six days.'

So Joshua's soldiers marched around Jericho
as God had said. No one made a noise,
except for the priests on their trumpets.

Then, on the seventh day, God said, 'This time you shall all march around the city seven times. And on the seventh time, when the priests blow their trumpets, this is a signal for everyone to shout as loud as they can.'

The people obeyed God. At the signal they stomped, screamed and shouted, and the walls of Jericho came tumbling down! Joyfully, the soldiers rushed in, and took the city. It was a great victory for God and his people!

We were tricked

Roar till you're sore

Our trust in God was rewarded

Hurrah!

Now we're shouting with happiness

Victory for God

We've won

THE MIRACLE OF NAAMAN'S CURE
2 Kings 5:1-14

Naaman was a commander in the Syrian army.
He was a very brave man, but he was also a leper.

One day, Naaman's wife was talking to her maid,
who came from Israel. 'In Israel, there is a man
of God called Elisha,' the maid said.
'He is a prophet and can heal Naaman.'

Naaman was excited when he heard this.
He asked the king of Syria if he could visit Elisha.
The king agreed.

16

'I shall send a letter and gifts to the king of Israel to tell him you're coming,' the king replied.

But when the king of Israel received the letter, he was angry. 'What does Naaman expect, miracles?' he gasped. 'I can't heal leprosy!' Elisha was listening. 'God can!' he said. 'Let Naaman come.'

When Naaman arrived, Elisha didn't meet him, he just sent a message saying: 'Wash in the River Jordan seven times and you will be healed.'

Now Naaman was furious. 'Have I come all this way for that!' he spluttered. 'I can wash in any old river back home!' He thought that Elisha would at least pray to God to heal him. Naaman turned to go, but his servants stopped him.

Give it a try

Trust him

Elisha knows best

What a wasted journey

'Elisha speaks for God,' they said. 'Do as he asks.'
So Naaman bathed in the River Jordan seven times
and his leprosy was cured! 'It's a miracle!' he shouted
– and he believed in God.

21

THE MIRACLE OF THE FIERY FURNACE
Daniel 3

King Nebuchadnezzar ruled in the ancient city of Babylon. He built himself a huge and beautiful golden statue.

'See this statue,' King Nebuchadnezzar said to the people. 'Every time you hear music of any kind, you must kneel down and worship it!
Whoever disobeys my command
will be thrown into
a fiery furnace!'

Of course, no one wanted to be thrown into the furnace. So whenever any person heard music – day or night – they quickly knelt to worship the statue.

However, three men from Israel called Shadrach, Meshach and Abednego refused to obey the command.
'We're not worshipping a statue!' they said.
'We serve only God in heaven.'

King Nebuchadnezzar was furious at this. 'Worship my statue or there will be trouble!' he cried. But Shadrach and his friends refused. 'Our God can even save us from the fiery furnace,' they replied. 'We trust him.'

The king's anger grew. 'Stoke the furnace up high,' he told his servants, 'and throw these men in!'

As soon as this was done, King Nebuchadnezzar looked through the furnace door and he gasped. Shadrach, Meshach and Abednego were unharmed, and with them was a fourth man who looked like an angel! It was God, protecting them.

Amazed, the king set the three men free.
'God saved us,' Shadrach said joyfully.
'Not a hair on our heads was singed.
Praise God!'

THE MIRACLE OF GOD TODAY

God still does miracles. If you listen carefully, you can hear his voice, deep inside you – talking to you.

This is your conscience. By it, God shows you right from wrong. Just think, God himself speaks to you, showing you the best way to live.
Isn't that a wonderful miracle!

First published in 1997 by
KEVIN MAYHEW LTD
Rattlesden
Bury St Edmunds
Suffolk IP30 0SZ

© 1997 Kevin Mayhew Ltd

The right of Claire Freedman to be identified as the author
of this work has been asserted by her in accordance
with the Copyright, Designs and Patents Act 1988.

All rights reserved. No part of this publication may be reproduced,
stored in a retrieval system, or transmitted, in any form
or by any means, electronic, mechanical, photocopying,
recording or otherwise, without the prior
written permission of the publisher.

0 1 2 3 4 5 6 7 8 9

ISBN 0 86209 983 8
Catalogue No 1500108

Front cover designed by Graham Johnstone
Illustrated by Arthur Baker
Typesetting by Louise Hill
Printed and bound in Great Britain